Kakuzo Okakura

Japan

described and illustrated by the Japanese

Kakuzo Okakura

Japan
described and illustrated by the Japanese

ISBN/EAN: 9783742823311

Manufactured in Europe, USA, Canada, Australia, Japa

Cover: Foto ©Andreas Hilbeck / pixelio.de

Manufactured and distributed by brebook publishing software
(www.brebook.com)

Kakuzo Okakura

Japan

JAPAN

DESCRIBED AND ILLUSTRATED BY THE JAPANESE

Written by

Eminent Japanese Authorities and Scholars

Edited by Captain F Brinkley of Tokyo Japan

SECTION ONE

PUBLISHED BY

J·B MILLET COMPANY

BOSTON MASS U S A

JAPAN.

I

THE EMPIRE; ITS SIZE, BUILDINGS, CITIES AND SCENERY.

APAN, since the resumption of her intercourse with Western nations forty years ago, has attracted multitudes of foreign tourists, and has inspired an extraordinarily large number of them to write books about her beauties and her quaintnesses. Not one of these many authors has been wholly condemnatory. Most of them found something to admire in the manners and customs of her people, and all have been charmed by her scenery. Certainly in the matter of seascape and landscape Nature has been profusely kind to the Isles of Nippon. They rise out of the sea with so many graces of form, and lie bathed in an atmosphere of such sparkling softness, that it is easy to sympathize with the legend ascribing their origin to crystals dropped from the point of the creator's spear. That they fell from some heaven of generous gods is a theory more consonant with their aspect than the sober fact that they form part of a great ring welded by volcanic energy in the Pacific Ocean, and that still, from time to time they shudder with uneasy memories of the fiery forces that begot them. Eastern Asia thrusts two long, slender arms into far Oriental waters: Kamtchatka in the north, Malacca in the south; and between these lies a giant girdle of islands holding in its embrace Siam, Cochin China, the Middle Kingdom, Korea and the eastern end of the Great White Czar's dominions, thus extending from latitude 50° north to the equator. When Commodore Perry anchored at Uraga in 1854 the empire of Japan stretched along two fifths of this girdle. Beginning on the south at Cape Sata, the lowest point of the Island of the Nine Provinces (Kiushu), it ended, on the north, with a disputed fragment of Saghalien and an unsettled number of the attenuated filament of islets called the Kuriles. Since then the empire has been pushed ten degrees southward. Now, including the Riukiu (Loochoo) Islands and Formosa, it constitutes three fifths of the girdle—a distance of two thousand miles— and extends over thirty degrees of latitude and thirty-five of longitude. Its expansion has followed the law of geographical affinities, temporarily transgressed in the case of the United States only, and ultimately to be verified by their history also,—south

I

ward the star of empire has taken its way. One loss of territory, however, was suffered by Japan in that interval, perhaps by way of permanent punishment for standing so long aloof from the outer world; she had to surrender to Russia the island of Saghalien—Karafuto, as her people call it. Saghalien forms a kind of territorial link between Japan and Russia.

A GROUP OF JAPANESE NOBLES AND DIGNITARIES.

Its northwestern coast almost feels the current of the Amur debouching at Nikolaievsk, and Yezo on its south is within easy rowing distance. Naturally Russians from the Amur region and Japanese from Yezo found their way to the island and pushed forward until their "spheres of influence" overlapped. Complications arose, and Japan, then almost powerless for offence or de-

fence in so remote and inhospitable a part of her dominions, found her people harassed and her settlements destroyed by Russian men-of-war. These were not acts of wanton aggression, Russia's ultimate purpose being to establish commercial relations with her neighbor. Perhaps Japan may be excused for hesitating to court the closer acquaintance of a people whom she knew only as incendiaries and raiders. At all events she hesitated so long that when at last (1875) she made up her mind to settle the question Saghalien had already been almost entirely colonized by Russian subjects, and its exchange for the northern islands of the inhospitable Kuriles seemed the sole exit from the dilemma. Assuredly this was not a profitable exchange for Japan, but it constituted a fitting sequel to her protracted and inveterate squabbles with Russia—squabbles that began in 1790 and taught the Japanese to regard the great Northern Power with distrust that recent events have not tended to dispel. Possibly instructed by her Saghalien experience, Japan took care that no other islands of questionable ownership within easy reach of her shores should remain a bait to aggressive appetites.

In 1871 she sent a commissioner and a body of colonists to take formal possession of the Bonin group, known to her as Ogasawara-jima, which, though discovered by her mariners nearly two hundred years previously, had not hitherto been included within her sphere of active occupation. But on the south, forming a series of stepping-stones between her territory and

Formosa, stretched a cluster of islands not to be so easily dealt with. They were the Riukiu group, called by the outside world the Luochoo, or Lewchew. Commodore Perry, whose patriotic sentiment often took the form of a desire to acquire "ports of refuge" in the East, strongly urged the United States government to adopt that course with regard to suitable harbors in Riukiu and the Bonins, and it is probable that his suggestion would have been acted on had his mission to Japan provoked any rough reception. But the fate of the Riukiu Islands was not to be so easily settled. Japan, indeed, never permitted herself to doubt that the islands were her property. They had long been regarded as an appanage of the Satsuma fief, among whose revenues their yearly taxes were counted. Their people spoke a language having close affinities with that of Japan, and their manners and customs showed an even more marked relationship. But they paid tribute to China, and the latter maintained toward them a demeanor of unpractical proprietorship. Not many years after the centralization of administrative authority in Japan and the abolition of feudalism, an event occurred that subjected the claims of the two powers to a conclusive test. A Riukiuan junk was cast away upon the coast of Formosa, and the crew were foully murdered by the Formosans. The Japanese government, at once assuming with regard to Riukiu the protective obligations of a sovereign, summoned China to punish her Formosan subjects and compensate the families of the murdered sailors. China resorted to her usual tactics of evasion. Instead of challenging Japan's attitude toward Riukiu, she sought rather to shuffle out of her own responsibility for the doings of the Formosans, so that, after a sufficient exercise of patience, Japan undertook the punitive duty herself, and sent a military expedition to Formosa to exact reparation *in loco*. This happened in 1874. It was the most suggestive event in Japan's modern history That she herself interpreted it to mean war with her big neighbor, no one living in the country at the time and observing the shock of patriotic excitement that thrilled the whole nation could for a moment doubt. Yet Japan was in no sense equipped for such a contest. Her new administration was not yet fully organized; her finances had not emerged from the confusion consequent upon transferring the accounts of the numerous fiefs to one central ledger her army was still in an embryonic stage; she had virtually no navy, nor any resources of marine transport; her treasury was almost empty, and her credit stood low. Nevertheless she did not shrink from the severest test of her sense of national responsibility, and if the spirit that she displayed was not rightly construed by the world at the time, it was because Western statesmen did not think the subject worthy of careful attention. As for the Pekin government, they had no fancy for fighting, and when Great Britain stepped in to mediate China readily agreed to indemnify Japan, provided that she withdrew her expeditionary force from Formosa. But the Riukiu problem had now been carried into the field of practical politics, and its solution threatened to involve an interminable controversy. General Grant, visiting the East in the course of his tour round the world in 1879, found the governments in Tokyo and Pekin as far as ever from an understanding. He suggested a partition of the islands in dispute, and Japan readily agreeing, negotiations on that basis were opened in the Chinese capital.

It had not yet been proved by experience that every evidence of a foreign state's willingness to compromise is invariably construed by China as a sign of weakness. When

A WINTER SCENE IN TOYOHAMA

a convention for the division of the islands had been drafted and signed by the plenipotentiaries of the two empires, the Chinese government turned around and declared in effect that no plenary powers had been vested in their representative, and that the document must be submitted for examination and, if need be, amendment at the hands of two other high officials. Thereupon the Japanese plenipotentiary left Pekin, and the Riukiu Islands were finally incorporated into the empire of Japan under the title of Okinawa Prefecture. China pigeon-holed her grievance, but before she found any easy opportunity to air it with effect the Korean question and the war precipitated by it in 1894 dwarfed all previous problems into insignificance. In the sequel of that war, Japan added Formosa and the Pescadores to her dominions, which thus consist now of five large islands and a multitude of islets, the latter scattered along her coasts or grouped into four clusters, the Kuriles (Chi-shima), on the north; the Bonins (Ogasawara-jima), on the east; the Loochoo (Riukiu or Okinawa), on the south, and the Pescadores, off the southwest coast of Formosa. The total area of these islands and islets is 162,000 square miles in round numbers, of which 16,000 square miles have been added since the centralization of the government in 1867. Taken in order of magnitude, the five principal islands are Hondo, or Nippon (86,294 square miles), Yezo (30,000 square miles), Formosa (13,982 square miles), Kiushu (13,763 square miles), and Shikoku (6,854 square miles). Previously to the acquisition of Formosa, the area of the Japanese empire was equal to that of the British Isles, Holland and Belgium combined. With the addition of Formosa and the Pescadores, it has become approximately equal to the area of the British Isles, Holland, Belgium and Denmark. It is noteworthy that the extension has been wholly southward, whatever diminution has taken place is on the north. The facts that Japan's *début* upon the stage of the world has been the signal for her territorial expansion; that the direction of her growth is southward; that her resources are now, for the first time, in process of rapid development; that her people, fired with national enthusiasm and permeated from highest to lowest with military spirit, entertain one absorbing ambition, to make their country the leading Power in the Orient; that she has shown extraordinary capacity for assimilating whatever is good and serviceable in Western civilization, and that her modern enterprises, though wholly unguided by experience, have in every case been successful—these facts impart vivid interest to the next chapters of her history. There are, indeed, some modifying considerations not without significance. These will be noted in their proper place; but the general situation seems to be summed up in the above statement.

From time immemorial Japan has been tormented by earthquakes. She thrills with volcanic energy. Since the seventh century of our era, destructive visitations of this nature figure with painful perpetuity in her records. They seldom attain the dimensions of a national catastrophe, but at intervals, happily growing longer, terrible destruction of life and property has to be laid to their account. Since the days when all striking exhibitions of natural force were attributed to supernatural agencies, the people of Japan have been accustomed to speak of a gigantic fish that lashes their coasts in moments of fury and sets the ocean

rolling shoreward in mountains. There is a measure of truth in this, as in every expression of popular observation. For it is from the direction of the sea that the seismic visit generally comes. Pendent from the great chain of volcanoes that stretches from the Kuriles to the Andamans, a heavy loop lies buried in the Pacific off the Izumi promontory on the mideastern coast

A STREET IN ENOSHIMA.

of the main island. In the craters of this loop are generated the forces that shock Japan with greatest intensity. The islands themselves have few active volcanoes, or "fire mountains" (*kwazan*), as the people call them. Neither does it appear that the active volcano is greatly to be dreaded as a source of seismic violence. The forces steadily dissipated by its continuous display of energy become dangerous only when, tamped in subterranean mines, they suddenly seek exit upwards along lines of least resistance, the loosely packed tunnels of extinct volcanoes. A vivid illustration of this theory was furnished ten years ago by a mountain called Bandaisan. During eleven centuries the volcano had been quiescent. Stalwart forests had crept upwards to the edge of its once steaming crater; villages had been built in the now verdure-clad scars torn by its ancient violence, and to a thermal spring bubbling within a stone's throw of the summit, invalids flocked, season after season, thoughtless of any ill greater than their own ailments. But one morning a volcanic mine exploding, without any previous notice, in the bowels of the mountain, tore away its whole northern face and discharged into space seven hundred million tons of rocks and earth, every particle of the colossal deluge rushing forward as though it had been shot from a cannon. Of the appalling results to life and property it is needless to speak; they have been recorded often enough. These resurrections of long deceased volcanoes are the most awful of seismic phenomena. Next to them in destructive suddenness are waves hurled against the shore by submarine volcanoes, playing with towns and hamlets as the storm plays with dead leaves, and strewing long reaches of coast with mangled corpses. Such a wave invaded the northeastern shore of the main island in June, 1896, just sixty years after the same region had suffered from a similar calamity. Yet there are evidences that Japan is gradually acquiring immunity from these calamities. They grow fewer and farther between with the lapse of centuries. Kyoto, for example, used to be notably subject to destructive shocks, but for sixty-five years it has remained comparatively safe. Tokyo's period of security has not been so long—only forty-six years. But during the whole of that time scarcely a dozen habitations have been wrecked by earthquakes. On the other hand, no city in Japan has had such awful experiences. In 1703 thirty-seven thousand of its citizens were crushed under falling houses or choked by huge waves. In 1855 fully twice as many perished, and some seventeen thousand buildings were shattered or burned.

It might be supposed that, living under the menace of such catastrophes, the Japanese people would be tormented by constant apprehension, and that their uneasiness would manifest itself in their daily life. To some extent that is the case. Their dwelling houses, for example, are always light wooden structures, sufficiently elastic to yield to forces which, if rigidly resisted, would be instantaneously destructive. One result of this necessity is that the higher efforts of architectural genius have found in Japan no field for their display. Architectural decoration, indeed, has been carried to great lengths, and a roof curve of singular grace has been evolved. But these beauties are confined to sacred buildings and to the houses of the nobility. A Japanese city is little better than a collection of shanties, and at intervals in the wooden shutters (*amado*, literally, rain-doors) that surround every veranda during the night, hinged panels are inserted to afford easy exit at the first vibration of an earthquake, for the shutters themselves, being slid consecutively into their places and bolted

MOUNT FUJI AS SEEN FROM KASHIWABARA.

Fuji, often called Fuji-san, Fuji-no-yama and Fusiyama, is the loftiest and most famous mountain in Japan. Its altitude has been variously estimated at from 12,234 to 12,490 feet above the sea. It stands in the centre of a great plain, about fifteen miles from the coast. Its vast bulk dominates the surrounding country, and its snow-clad peak may be seen by the approaching mariner long before the coast line appears above the horizon. Although now quiescent, Fuji must still be accounted a volcano. History records several violent eruptions, the latest being in 1707. It is quite practicable to make an ascent to the summit between the latter part of July and before the middle of September, but at any other time the peak is inaccessible.

by a somewhat intricate contrivance, cannot be hastily removed. But apart from these special accommodations, the Japanese seem to take little thought for the perils by which nature
has surrounded them. They laughingly catalogue the four most formidable factors of every-
day existence as "earthquakes, thunderbolts, fires, and fathers" (*jishin, kaminari, kwaji,
oyaji*), the classification itself evincing the spirit in which it is made. Probably no people in
the world take the goods that the gods send more gleefully or the evils more philosophically.
It has been calculated that the capital, Tokyo, is laid in ashes once in every quarter of a century; that is to say, the houses destroyed there by fire in twenty-five years aggregate the
number comprising the whole city. The steam fire-engine has disturbed that estimate, but it
was true once, and it remains a truth to a majority of the citizens. They comprehend its
significance. The clanging of the fire-bell night after night, and sometimes time after time
in the same night, throughout the winter, means that, in hundreds of cases, competence
hardly earned by years of patient industry is converted into penury by the fire-demon in as
many minutes. Yet they call fire the "flower of the capital," and ridicule the notion that any
one timid of such happenings should reside in the great city. There is no bravado in their
mood. They act as they speak. Women and children, seated in a temporary shelter beside
the smoking ruins of their homes, begin the day after their misfortune as they began the day
that preceded it. Their circumstances have changed, but their duty remains unaltered—to
bear their own share of
the sorrow without ever
intruding their burden
upon the notice of others.
Yet it is a pitiable
thought that the growth
of wealth should be re-
tarded by such catastro-
phes. The earthquake
is at the root of the evil.
It dictates the use of
flame-fuel for building
material, thus inviting
conflagrations, forbid-
ding architectural effort,
denuding the people's

THE NAGARA-GAWA BRIDGE AFTER THE GREAT EARTHQUAKE IN 1891.

homes of all valuables that are not immediately portable, and invading their lives with
heart-breaking losses. During the era of enlightenment that commenced with the abolition of feudalism and the centralization of the government in 1867—the *Meiji* era, as it is
called—earthquakes were, for the first time, brought within the field of scientific research in

Japan. A seismological society was formed, originally at the instance of foreign experts but ultimately under Japanese auspices, and investigations were conducted with much energy and ability. Summing up the results obtained by long years of effort, we find that the inquiry has not yet emerged from its preliminary stage. The principal achievement has been the construction of seismographs capable of accurately registering the direction and force of earth movements. It has been demonstrated practically, as it might have been foretold theoretically, that, to resist the destructive effects of a shock, houses must be built so that the oscillations of all their connected parts shall be synchronous; brick chimneys, for example, not being rigidly attached to wooden roofs of which the inertia is markedly smaller. It has also been shown that a deep trench surrounding an edifice interrupts, and therefore mitigates, the transmission of the seismic force, and that, in the case of a city covering so extended an area as Tokyo, difference of locality produces a palpable difference in the intensity with which an earthquake makes itself felt. Seismic maps of all the principal centres of residence throughout the empire ought, therefore, to be of prime importance for site-selecting purposes. But life is short and the mischievous earthquake a rare visitor. These niceties of contrivance and delicacies of forethought do not commend themselves to the average Japanese. He is content to be guided by the empirical tradition that, as the bending bamboo springs straight after the blast, so the light wooden structure that yields a little to the seismic thrust is much more likely to survive than the solid edifice that attempts to rigidly resist an irresistible force. In obedience to that creed his towns and cities have everywhere grown up in almost squalid insignificance. The dwellings of the non-official classes are assemblies of pigmy structures, never relieved by stately façade, lordly portico or towering steeple. Moreover, unlike the Chinese, no Japanese builder has ever thought of decorating the front of a store or place of business with broad panels of polychrome carvings, or other architectural gewgaws, to invite the ravages of the elements and present, after a few seasons, an aspect of battered dilapidation more suggestive of perishability than even the flimsy edifices themselves. The Japanese loves simplicity. If nature's waywardness has imposed on him the necessity of living in a frail and lowly dwelling, his innate good taste saves him from the solecism of attempting to disguise the unwelcome necessity by incongruous devices. Nothing could be more frankly unpretentious than the clusters of lowly buildings that constitute his towns, and nothing more striking than the contrast between these structures and the massive edifices that are gradually rising into existence under the impulse of the country's imported civilization. At first, Japan was content to administer her new laws, carry on her new education, and transact the affairs of her newly organized State in wooden buildings either of the old type, or of a hybrid character, cheap, indeed, but shockingly unsightly. Hundreds, nay thousands, of this latter class of building may still be seen in the official capitals of all the provincial communes; rudimentary, rectangular structures, without veranda, balcony or any projection to break the bald uniformity of their faces.

They are the communal schools, or telegraph and post offices, or, it may be, police bar racks No effort has been made to harmonize them with their environment. They disfigure the landscape, and suggest what happily is not true, that the alien systems taught or pursued within their walls have not yet been assimilated into the life of the nation. But

in the great cities, espe cially in Tokyo,[1] it is dif ferent. There structures worthily representative of the *Meiji* civilization are rapidly springing up: solid piles of brick and stone, state departments, courts of law, banks, municipal edifices, min isterial residences, ho tels, clubs, and so forth. Side by side with these the wooden dwellings and stores of the city proper shrink into still

AN INFORMAL VISIT.

more dwarf-like insignificance, so that it were difficult to find elsewhere a national capital with streets more absolutely devoid of beautiful, stately or dignified features. The citi zens, however, are fired with picturesque ambition. Ten years ago they devised a mag nificent plan of broadened streets, spacious parks and regenerated edifices. The city that was to rise from these projects became known as the "Tokyo of dreamland." It has not yet emerged into the region of reality. Here and there only, the streets have been widened. Whenever one of the frequent conflagrations lays a street in ruins, the new houses are pushed far back from their old sites, with the result that in the poorest quarters, where fires are most common, some of the streets have now assumed grand proportions. But the houses themselves remain as insignificant as ever, and, of course, since every widening of a thoroughfare ought to be accompanied by a proportionate increase in the dimensions of the buildings that stand on either side of it, the process of Tokyo's so-called "improvement" seems retrogressive from an artistic standpoint. Kyoto (population 230,000), the ancient capital, presents in some respects a similar character, though as yet the humility of its archi tecture has not been so palpably accentuated by contrast with modern structures of over shadowing dimensions. During eleven centuries Kyoto was the seat of Japanese Imperial ism ; during three, Tokyo was the stronghold of the Tokugawa Regents. In an Occidental

[1] Circumference 30 miles, and area 100 square miles, including all the suburbs ; population 1,301,376.

State all the advantages of wealth, size and magnificence might be expected to belong to the Imperial city. But in Japan, while the Emperor governed after a nominal fashion, the Regent, or *Shogun*, as he was called, exercised the whole administrative power; and whereas the nobles that frequented the Court in Kyoto were men of scant incomes and limited influence, the feudal chiefs that took their orders direct from the *Shogun* possessed large wealth and were virtually supreme within the limits of their fiefs. This difference may be read in the features of the two cities. Throughout the whole of the Western Capital *Sai-kyo*, or Kyoto, as distinguished from Tokyo, the Eastern Capital there is not to be found a solitary residence that could be associated, by any stretch of imagination, with opulent ownership. The palace itself is severely simple. Decorative paintings, from the brushes of some great artists, and the finely grained, knotless timbers of which it is built, alone entitle it to be called something better than a mere shelter from the elements. As for the houses of the court nobles the *Kuge*, every one of whom could trace his descent directly from an occupant of the throne their structure and environment are eloquent of straitened incomes, if not of actual poverty. It is true that when (794 A. D.) Kyoto was chosen for the Imperial capital, the Emperor ruled as well as governed, and the plan of the new metropolis was traced with a grandeur of conception upon which Japanese historians love to descant. The streets were laid out with mathematical precision, a vast network of communications, comprised within a rectangle at the centre of whose northern face stood the Imperial citadel. The Kyoto of that era was undoubtedly a city magnificent according to the standard of its epoch, and that the daily life of its citizens was permeated by a degree of refinement and civilization unknown in Europe at the time, there are ample evidences to show. But architecturally it had no claim to be called grand, and as conflagration after conflagration laid its imperial citadel and its streets in ashes, edifices less and less pretentious rose from the ruins. For with the development of feudalism and the decentralization of the administrative power, wealth flowed from the capital to the provinces, and though the former remained always the centre of whatever was aristocratic, refined or artistic in the realm, the sovereign and his courtiers had to engage in a constant struggle to make ends meet, and the loyalty of the citizens constrained them to adapt the dimensions of their residences and the outward fashions of their lives to the lowly examples set by the Emperor and his aristocracy. In Tokyo, on the other hand, all the puissance and opulence of the empire's real ruler impressed themselves on the official quarter of the city. Round the castle of the *Shogun* a triple line of huge fosses stretched, the outermost measuring nine and a half miles in length, the innermost one and a half, their scarps built up with colossal blocks of granite, carried hundreds of miles over sea and set in place by labor employing contrivances that must have been primitive at so remote an epoch,

the beginning of the seventeenth century, but were yet capable of achieving results wonderful to contemplate even today. Above these grand masses of masonry were piled

great banks of earth, their slopes turfed with fine Korean grass, and their summits planted
with pine trees, trained year after year to stretch evergreen arms towards the spacious moats,
varying in width from one hundred and seventy yards to twenty-two, through which flowed
broad sheets of water, reaching the city by cunningly planned aqueducts from a river twenty

miles distant. There is
not to be found else-
where in the world a
more stupendous monu-
ment of military power,
and if any one consider-
ing such a work, as well
as its immediate prede-
cessor, the equally colossal stronghold of the
great *Taiko*, in Osaka,
and its numerous con-
temporaries of lesser but
still striking proportions
in the principal fiefs,
refuses to credit the

FANCLUN MAKERS.

Japanese mind with capacity for mighty conceptions, and the Japanese brain with competence
to plan and carry out great undertakings, he must be either prejudiced or deficient in the
deductive faculty. In this cyclopean fortress of Tokyo there is also to be seen the unswerving
homage to the beautiful that holds every Japanese a worshipper at nature's shrine, even
when he seems to rely most implicitly on his own resources of brain and muscle. Placid
lakes lapping the feet of stupendous battlements; noble pines bending over their own graceful reflection in still waters; long stretches of velvety sward making a perpetual presence of
rustic freshness among the dust and moil of city life; flocks of soft-plumaged wild fowl
placidly sailing in the moats or sunning themselves on the banks, careless of the tumult and
din of the streets overhead; sheets of lotus bloom glowing in the shadow of grim counter-
scarps—where but in Japan can we find so deliberate and so successful an effort to convert
the frowns of a fortress into the smiles of a garden? This castle of the Tokugawa Regents
is a portion of the alphabet by which we may read Japanese character. Hidden beneath a
passion for everything graceful and refined there is a strong yearning for the pageant of war
and for the dash of deadly onset; and just as the Shogun sought to display before the eyes of
the citizens of his capital a charming picture of gentle peace, though its setting was a frame-
work of vast military preparation, so the Japanese of every era has loved to turn from the
fencing-school to the arbor, from the field of battle to the society of the rockery and the

cascade, delighting in the perils and struggles of the one as much as he admires the graces and repose of the other. In another manner, also, feudalism left its impress upon the eastern capital of the empire; for, in order to insure the allegiance of the great provincial barons, they were required to reside in Tokyo — or Yedo, as it was then called — every second year;

A TAILOR AT REST.

and when, in obedience to this order, each chieftain began to build for himself, his family and his army of retainers an urban residence and a suburban, there sprang up a constructive rivalry that soon enriched the city and its environs with a great number of picturesque parks and spacious mansions. The average citizen, indeed, saw little of the beauty of these places; there was no access for him within their walled and carefully guarded enclosures. But during the two and a half centuries of their existence Tokyo was a veritable city of gardens, all laid out with consummate skill and tended with loving care. The labor expended upon this work must have been enormous. Every rock — and the Japanese landscape-gardener uses a profusion of rocks — rocks for the margins of lakes; rocks for the beds of cascades; rocks to push their shoulders from hill and shrubbery, and rocks to form paths across parterres — every rock had to be brought by ship from distant provinces. They were no mere bowlders that two or three men might lift, but portly masses of stone, weighing, sometimes, tens of tons, and having to be dragged to their ornamental resting-places by hundreds of shouting coolies and teams of straining oxen. Inside these parks, created at such a lavish outlay of care and cost, stood houses that were miracles of the joiner's skill and the lumberman's craft, where the representatives of military feudalism lived lives of refined indulgence, amid works of art, transitions of flowery seasons, rustlings of silken robes, contests of rhythmical concerts, and, sometimes, shocking catastrophes. No element of war or arms seemed to obtrude itself into the luxurious languor of their existence, except that, flanking the great gate of the *yashiki* and stretching occasionally around three sides of the enclosure, stood long, low buildings, their outward faces pierced at rare intervals by strongly barred windows, and the chief article of furniture in all their rooms a sword-rack. These *nagaya* were the barracks of each baron's men at-arms, and up to the fall of feudalism so many streets were bordered by edifices of that ominous type, and such a multitude of their inmates were to be met striding along, a pair of razor-edged swords in their girdles and the pride of arms in their mien, that for all the pretty parks and dainty mansions of the nobles, for all the disguise of soft sward and tender-sprayed pines that overlay the grimness of the central castle's battlements, Tokyo could never be mistaken for anything but what it was, the citadel of a military system embracing all the warlike resources of a battle-loving nation. At the Restoration of 1867, when the Tokugawa Regents were stripped of their power, when feudalism was abolished, and the Emperor resumed the administration of State affairs, an era of destruction set in. Stripped of their revenues and no longer required to reside in the capital, the majority of the barons left their Tokyo residences to be sold or dismantled, and among the men that had planned and were now directing these great political changes none had leisure or means to think of acquiring mansions and parks such as only wealthy nobles could be justified in maintaining. With a few exceptions the parks disappeared. Denuded of everything salable, — rocks, shrubs, timber, — their buildings burned or pulled to pieces, their enclosing walls levelled with the ground, they became simply so many vacant spaces, breaking the continuity of the city and imparting to it an aspect of unsightly irregularity.

It will be seen from what has been written here that in ancient as well as in modern times two Tokyos have to be distinguished — official Tokyo and commercial Tokyo. It is to the latter, or Tokyo proper, that reference is made when the buildings are described as insignificant and almost squalid, their general aspect suggesting a state of poverty and business stagnation in strange contrast with the cheerful faces, comfortable garments and

FOOT BRIDGE ACROSS THE MIYANOSHITA RIVER.

easy-going ways of the citizens. This dual nature of the capital is a true reflection of the nation's social structure in former times, and to a lesser but still considerable degree in the present era. The Japanese have always been divided into two distinct classes, — patricians, *shizoku*, or the military class, as they are commonly called; and commoners, *heimin*, or ordinary folks; the numerical ratio between them being as one to twelve approximately. The patricians had a monopoly of the administrative and military power; the commoners had only to till the soil, take fish out of the seas and rivers, and conduct the vulgar operations of trade and barter. From the pageant of war, from the sweets of office, from the pride of rank, from the arena of intellectual competition, the *heimin* were completely excluded. Their lives were as subordinate to those of the *shizoku* as their lowly dwellings were overshadowed by the latter's massive castles. This gulf of separation was not always so wide. Its dimensions grew with the development of military feudalism, and its growth is accurately represented in the leading features of the two capitals. When Kyoto became the metropolis of the empire, distinctions of caste had not yet been sharply accentuated by the supremacy of the sword. The mass of the people still lived close to their sovereign, figuratively speaking, and strategical considerations did not imperatively limit the choice of sites for the Imperial capital. There was virtual freedom of selection, except that custom had long dictated separate residences for the Emperor and the Heir Apparent—a custom common in Occidental countries, and still observed in Japan, with this modification, however, that whereas the sovereign and his apparent successor now reside in the same city, the rule formerly was to choose wholly different localities. Of course it resulted that there grew up about the palace of the prince material interests and moral associations opposed to a change of habitation, and thus, on his accession to the throne, he usually transferred the capital of the empire from the place occupied by his predecessor to the site of his own palace. In addition to this source of frequent change, it happened occasionally that the residence of the Imperial Court, and therefore the capital of the empire, was moved from one place to another twice or even thrice during the same reign, the only limit set to all these shiftings being that the five adjacent provinces occupying the waste of the main island, and known as "Gokinai," were regarded as possessing some prescriptive title to contain the seat of government, Yamato being especially honored in that respect. A long list might be compiled of places distinguished by Imperial residence during the early centuries, notable among them being Kashiwara, the capital of the Emperor Jimmu; Naniwa (now Osaka), that of the Emperor Nintoku; Otsu, that of the Emperor Tenchi; and Fujiwara, that of the Emperor Temmu. It must be noted, however, that in those ages of comparative simplicity and frugality the seat of government was not invested with attributes of pomp and grandeur such as the haughtier conceptions of later generations prescribed. The sovereign's mode of life differed little from that of his subjects, and the transfer of his residence from place to place involved no costly or disturbing effect. But as civilization progressed; as the population grew; as the business of administration became more complicated; as increasing intercourse with China furnished new standards for measuring the interval between ruler and ruled, and, above all, as class distinctions acquired emphasis, the character of the palace assumed magnificence proportionate to the Imperial ceremonies and national receptions that had to be held there. It is

not easy to trace the gradual stages of this development, but it had certainly proceeded far
by the beginning of the eighth century, for the capital then established at Nara by the
Empress Gemmyo was on a scale of unprecedented magnitude and splendor. A lady's name
is fitly associated with this first payment of large tribute to outward appearances. Seven

sovereigns reigned at
Nara consecutively.
They were held there
from generation to gen-
eration partly by the
environment they them-
selves created, and
partly, no doubt, by a
perception of the advan-
tages accruing from a
thorough centralization
of the governing power.
But when the Emperor
Kwammu (782-805 A.D.)
ascended the throne, he
found that Nara was not

COOPERS AT WORK.

conveniently situated for administrative purposes, and after some uncertainty he finally
selected Uda, in Yamashiro province, and took steps to transfer his Court thither. The
event was invested with much ceremony, and was regarded as a subject of national rejoicing,
the people calling the capital *Heian jo*, or the "citadel of tranquillity." This is the modern
Kyoto. It continued to be the Imperial capital during a period of 1,074 years, though not
the seat of administrative authority; for from the establishment of military feudalism in the
twelfth century until its abolition in the sequel of the *Meiji* Restoration (1867) the sovereign
ruled in name only, the executive power being wielded in reality by a military regent who
had his own capital elsewhere. Seventy-seven Emperors held their courts successively in
Kyoto, with diminishing pomp and pageant as the centuries rolled by, but never with any
diminution of the sanctity attributed to them by their subjects. During an interval so protracted, the city, of course, underwent many changes, but to this day its general plan remains
on the lines of its earliest projection. It was built after the scheme of Nara, with modifica-
tions borrowed from the metropolis of the Tang dynasty in China. The outline was rectangular, 17,530 feet from north to south, and 15,080 feet from east to west. Moats and palisades
surrounded the whole,—the system of crenelated walls and flanking towers not having been
yet introduced,—and the Imperial palace, its citadel, administrative departments and assembly halls occupied the centre of the northern portion. The palace was approached from the

south, its main gate (*Shujaku mon*) opening upon a long street 280 feet wide (called *Shujaku oji*, or the Shujaku thoroughfare) which ran right down the centre of the city, terminating at the *Rajo* gate. The city was thus divided into two equal parts of which the eastern was designated *Sakyo*, or "left metropolis," and the western *Ukyo*, or "right metropolis."

The superficial division was into districts (*jo*) of which there were nine, all equal in size except those on the east and west of the palace. An elaborate system of subdivision was adopted. The unit or *ko* (house) was a space measuring 100 feet by 50. Eight of these units made a row (*gyo*); four rows, a street (*cho*); four streets, a division (*ho*); four divisions, a square (*bo*); and four squares, a district (*jo*). The entire capital contained 1,216 *cho* and 38,912 houses. The arrangement of the streets was strictly regular. They lay parallel and at right angles, like the lines on a checkerboard. The Imperial citadel measured 3,840 feet from east to west, and 4,600 feet from north to south. On each side were three gates; in the middle stood the palace, surrounded by the buildings of the various administrative depart-ments, and in front were the assembly and audience halls. The nine districts were divided from each other by streets, varying in width from 170 feet to 80 feet. They intersected the city from east to west, were numbered from 1 to 9, as *ichi jo, ni jo, san jo,* and so on — names retained until this day — and were themselves intersected in turn by similar streets running north and south, and by lanes at regular intervals. The buildings, as has been already stated, were lowly and insignificant. Even in the case of the palace the architects observed the austere canons of the *Shinto* cult, which prescribed purity and simplicity as the essential attributes of refinement; and in the case of the citizens' dwellings every effort to obtain lightness, airi-ness or ornamentation was reserved for cham-bers opening upon inner

KAGO BEARERS

courts, or looking out on miniature back gardens, so that the front effect was sombre and monotonous. Many of the houses were roofed with shingles, but some had slate-colored tiles, and the palace itself was rendered conspicuous by green glazed tiles imported from China. The conception of such a city at such an epoch — half a century before Lodbrok,

THE BRONZE BUDDHA AT KAMAKURA.

There are countless images of Buddha to be found throughout Japan, but none of them can for a moment compare with this great work of art, which stands facing the sea on the deserted site of Kamakura, an ancient capital of Japan. It is wonderfully impressive, not merely because of its size, but because it truly symbolizes the central idea of Buddhism — the intellectual calm which comes of perfected knowledge and the subjugation of all passion. To-day it stands in the open air, surrounded by a small park kept in order by private subscription. When built in 1251 it was under cover of a large temple 150 feet square. A tidal wave in 1369 destroyed the building, but left the statue unharmed. The temple was rebuilt and again destroyed by a second tidal wave in 1494, since which time the image has remained uncovered. It is, however, in excellent preservation, and will no doubt be able to resist the elements for centuries to come. The first temple erected on this spot was in the eighth century, but the temple which first sheltered the image was built in 1241.

The eyes of the Buddha are of pure gold, and the silver boss on the forehead weighs 30 pounds. The image is built of bronze castings brazed together, and the hollow interior contains a small shrine and a ladder leading up into the head. The dimensions are as follows:

	ft.	in.		ft.	in.
Height	49	7	Width of mouth	3	2
Circumference	97	2	Height of bump of wisdom		9
Length of face	8	5	Diameter of bump of wisdom	2	4
Width from ear to ear	17	9	Curls (of which there are 830).		
Round white boss on forehead	1	3	Height		9
Length of eye	3	11	Diameter	1	
Length of eyebrow	4	2	Length from knee to knee	35	8
Length of ear	6	6	Circumference of thumb	3	
Length of nose	3	9			

the Dane, sailed up the Seine, and fifty-five years before the birth of Alfred the Great bears eloquent testimony to the highly civilized condition of Japan and to the Emperor Kwammu's greatness of mind and resources. But the general plan of the capital teaches another lesson also: it shows that the residences of the people received as much consideration as the twenty two edifices comprised within the palace enclosure. Kyoto, in short, was the metropolis of the nation, not the central citadel of a military administration.

Tokyo's history is totally dissimilar. It was originally a mere fortress. The great natural fastness of Japan lies between a range of mountains of which Fujiyama is the crown and a network of rivers, of which the principal is the Tonegawa. Within this fastness the military regents established themselves. At first they were content to hold the passes of the mountains against possible attacks from the south. Their capital was then Odawara, a sea shore city lying inside the fastness and at the base of the mountains. By and by, however it became necessary to guard the river front also, and the first captain to whom that duty was intrusted, Ota Dokan, made Yedo his headquarters and constructed there a fortress des tined to be subsequently converted into the magnificent military stronghold described above This happened in the middle of the fifteenth century. There were no evidences then of the place's future greatness: a few fishermen's hamlets, an immense reedy plain, excellently suited for deploying troops, and a sweep of great rivers easy to hold against an enemy, these were the features that Ota found. Planning his fortress, he took no thought whatever for the people of the district.

Nearly a century and a half later (1590 A. D.), Ieyasu, the first of the Tokugawa Regents, in obedience to the order of the *Taiko*, made Yedo the capital of the eight provinces bestowed on him by that most illustrious of Japan's generals and statesmen. But in the eyes of Ieyasu also the place was nothing more than a military citadel. The colossal for tress erected by him covered all the best building sites, and had not the sea been gradually pushed back by the detritus of the three big rivers on the north, a city of a million inhabi tants could never have grown up at the foot of the Regent's huge fosses and under the shadow of his giant battlements. The castle has now become a mere residence; its massive gates removed, its tall flanking towers levelled with the ground; the barracks of its mensat arms replaced by sward and shrubbery. But simultaneously with the disappearance of these evidences of military supremacy, officialdom has reasserted the dominance of the *shizoku* by erecting for itself buildings that contrast almost as strikingly with the dwellings of the *heimin* as the Tokugawa stronghold contrasted with the humble city lying at its feet. That distinction recognized -- it can hardly be called a difference -- Tokyo is seen to reflect faith fully the political changes that Japan has undergone since mediaeval times: the transition from administration by the Emperor to administration by representatives of military feudal ism, and the transfer of the latter's power to a *shizoku* hegemony, which made modern Japan but still stands high above the mass of the nation it leads and governs. Kyoto, on the other hand, remains the capital of ancient Japan; its appearance typical of the quiet old times when rulers and ruled were as one family, and essentially typical of the genuine spirit of Japanese civilization, refinement without ostentation. It is true that gorgeous and imposing Buddhist temples confer exceptional distinction on the city. But these are, in a sense,

exotics, owing their magnificence of paraphernalia and wealth of decoration to the country where the creed was born. Everywhere the houses of the citizens present a modest though thoroughly neat appearance, their rusticity suggesting few graces of life until one passes within and finds that the humblest of these dwellings looks out at the back on a tiny park, with miniature waterfalls, toy hills and dwarf forests, and that, although the tide of industrial progress, with its grime and din, has not left this ancient city entirely uninvaded, the potter or enameller may still be seen decorating his vases or building up his subtle tracery of many-hued designs while the flowers and leaves that he copies look in at him through the windows of his workshop. To see in clear outlines the influence that has been exercised upon the life of the *heimin* by the advent of the new civilization that worships at the shrine of mammon, it is necessary to go to Osaka,[1] now the commercial capital of Japan. There the whole city is pervaded by an atmosphere of business, and gradually the movements of the citizens begin to betray the anxious haste of trading communities in the Occident. There has been a great growth of population, a great extension of the streets, a great access of wealth. But the prominent development seems to have been in the direction of factory chimneys. A thousand of these unsightly erections now look down upon a city where, a quarter of a century ago, not even one was to be seen; a canopy of smuts and smoke begins to replace the crystalline purity of the old-time atmosphere, and the sobbing of the steam-engine invades the laughter of the light-hearted citizens. Officialdom is absolutely unobtrusive, and the reservoir of the city's water works marks the site of Hideyoshi's feudal fortress.

One feature common, though not in an equal degree, to all Japanese towns is the

[1] Area, 8 square miles; population, 484,000.

absence of any dazzling display of wares in shop-fronts. That part of the vender's art remains little developed, doubtless because trade, having always been despised as the meanest of bread-earning professions, shrank from thrusting its evidences upon public notice. In Kyoto some of the largest and wealthiest stores are distinguishable only by the air of bustle that pervades their precincts, and even that used to be hidden from the aristocratic customer, who found himself ushered into a quiet chamber, opening upon shrubberies and rockeries, and with the most unbusiness-like aspect conceivable. These things have changed somewhat with the times, but there is still implicit obedience to the old canon that prescribes sobriety of exterior as an essential of good taste. Just as in a work of art the genuine Japanese artist seeks to supply details of decoration and technique that become visible only on close examination, so the Kyoto citizen builds his store in such a manner that whatever it contains of the admirable or the attractive becomes visible only on passing within. The visitor is astonished to find that a building seeming to consist altogether of a few weather-beaten boards and gloomy lattices forms the front of a spacious compound, within which are fireproof warehouses, neat and tasteful chambers, charming gardens, and show-rooms where a wealth of fine wares are arranged with excellent taste and skilful business instinct.

In Tokyo the methods of the tradesman are less consistent with the traditions of artistic modesty. The science of display without ostentation is not so well understood. It is true that the dealer keeps his choicest specimens and most valuable stock packed away in a fireproof "godown," whence he will not take the trouble to fetch anything specially fine or rare unless he diagnoses something of the connoisseur in his customer. Therein, however, his concession is not to good taste but to caution. As a matter of choice, he would prefer to marshal attractions in such a manner as to capture public attention, but whatever be the measure of his will, the results he obtains look wholly contemptible compared with the array of interesting and costly objects that deck the windows of an American or European store. It may seem, indeed, that the fault lies primarily with the shops, which, being sombre and of petty dimensions, cannot be easily adapted to exhibition purposes. But that is a feature rather than a cause. The whole art of inviting custom by appeals to the eye remains undeveloped in Japan, partly because it is opposed to the genius of the people, and partly because the low status of the merchant has hitherto condemned trade to a hole-and-corner existence. It is beginning now to raise its head, but long years must elapse before a Japanese city shows anything of the commercial glitter that characterizes an Occidental mart.

It does not fall within the scope of this work to speak at any length of the scenery of Japan. Innumerable writers have already descanted upon the beauties of the much-favored islands of the far Pacific, and so much eloquence has been devoted to describing their natural charms, that the reality can scarcely fail to disappoint any estimate founded on these panegyrics. Perhaps the most salient characteristic of the country is that its natural features remain, in great part, undisturbed by the hand of man. The Japanese are industrious and frugal. Theirs is not a land where the necessaries of life can be obtained without a struggle. Rice, the great staple of their food, is a cereal the cultivation of which involves toil of the hardest and least inviting description. Wherever an opportunity offers to enlist the bounty of nature it is eagerly utilized. Sailing through the Inland Sea, famous among all ocean inlets for the charms of its surroundings, one sees that every little spot of arable soil, whether on rocky island or steep hillside, has been attacked by the mattock of the indefatigable peasant, and that every cove shelters a hamlet whose inhabitants snatch a precarious living from sea and soil. Yet, despite these evidences of agricultural earnestness, it is a fact

A BUDDHIST FUNERAL.

that eighty-eight parts out of every hundred of the superficies of these nominally much-favored islands yield no food to the people. It is true that the cultivated area expands year by year, and that the expansion will probably continue as railways, roads and steamships bring new districts within reach of markets. But in this matter the responsibility rests not with the paucity of communications so much as with natural conditions. The state of soil that exists at the sites of some of the chief cities finds a parallel throughout the country at large. Just as the ashes and shards of repeated conflagrations have accumulated in the former case until the real subsoil is beyond profitable reach, so in the latter, volcanoes, bursting through the primitive rocks, have buried wide areas under deep shrouds of pumice, so that hill slopes and plains which ought to contribute generally to the nation's sustenance are not capable of nourishing anything better than bamboograss and stunted scrub. But if these volcanoes have impaired the productive qualities of the land, they have immensely enhanced its scenic beauties. The term volcano conveys, under ordinary circumstances, a suggestion of destruction, desolation, nakedness and disruption. Such features are not presented by the Japanese volcano. It is usually a mountain of soft contours, placid aspect and tender verdure. For, if nature created it in a hurry, she hastens also to subject it to climatic influences that rob it of all ruggedness and clothe it with abundant vegetation. In central Japan the traveller may find scenic sights of grandeur and wildness on an Alpine scale. But elsewhere the scenery is essentially gentle — green valleys lying nestled in the arms of softly sloping hills, groves of feathery bamboo and billow-boughed pines, fantastically indented seacoasts, where the waves seldom raise their voices above a whisper, an atmosphere of exquisite opalescence, and brooding over all a perpetual stillness that seems to be deepened rather than disturbed by the occasional note of sweet-toned temple bells. With such scenery one does not fall in love at first sight. Familiarity endears it. The newcomer must be disappointed if he looks to find at once everything that he has been taught to expect. But he may rest assured that at the last there will remain imprinted on his recollection a picture of satisfying beauty, although its components are not separately striking or its colors brilliant.

There are, indeed, two great wants, the glow of flowers and the song of birds. So conspicuously do flowers figure in Japanese decorative art, and so much has been written about the cherry-blossom and plum-blossom picnics of the people, about their flower symbols of the four seasons, their chrysanthemums, their peonies, their irises, and their wistaria, that their country presents itself to the imagination as a veritable garden of Hesperia, brilliant, beautiful and fragrant. But in truth the great value attached to flowers in Japan is due, not to their profusion, but to their paucity. There are no pastures dewed with daisies and starred with buttercup, dandelion and cowslip; no glades carpeted with bluebells; no golden plains of orange-scented gorse; no groves of laburnum and lilac; no fields of glowing poppies. With the exception of the azalea, not a single flowering shrub or plant is sufficiently gregarious to offer a wide expanse of blossom, and the azalea has its own favorite haunts, not here, there and everywhere, but only in special localities, few and far between. Nor is the bloom of the much-vaunted cherry and plum richer or more abundant in Japan than in the Occident. An American or English orchard displays in early summer a glory of blossom not to be surpassed by anything in the far East. The difference is this: that the cherry and plum, as fruits, being comparatively worthless in Japan, the flowers alone are prized, and great groves of trees are planted in places of popular resort for the sake of the grand but transient glow that they make in their season of bloom. Were the fruit valuable, the Japanese cultivator is far too practical to sacrifice it to display. His treatment of the pear proves this. The Japanese pear is a miserable fruit to Western palates: it is without succulence or flavor; a superior kind of turnip. It certainly possesses no merits that entitle it to careful culture. But every one eats it in Japan, and at every wayside stall it figures conspicuously among the autumn edibles. Therefore its flower is little accounted, but the tree itself is guarded in orchards, and thither visitors go when the pears are ripening, not when the flowers are in bloom. Yet a Japanese pear orchard presents a magnificent spectacle in May. Thousands of trees are planted at equal intervals, their boughs trained so as to spread laterally along a trellis of uniform height. Sometimes, as in the case of the Kawasaki orchard, midway between Tokyo and Yokohama, this trellis covers an area of many acres, and looking down on it in the blooming season, one sees a spread of blossom at once grand

and lovely. Such sights would certainly be included among the holiday delights of the nation were there no question of saving the flowers for the sake of the fruit. It is more than probable that in the Occident, also, if the plum, the cherry, the apple and the pear were not so pleasant to the palate, the trees that bear these fruits would obtain a new vogue on account of their flowers; would figure conspicuously in gardens instead of being relegated to orchards, and would be massed so as to form profuse glories of bloom in park and landscape. Thus we are reduced to the prosaic reflection that a very practical element lies at the root of the Japanese people's apparent worship of blossoms elsewhere counted commonplace: deprived of the fruit, they compensate themselves by making much of the flower. Still the fact remains that no other nation is so thoroughly permeated with the love of flowers. It is

A DEALER IN INLAID WOODENWARE.

curious to observe the almost intuitive recognition that this phase of the national disposition receives from comparative strangers. Fresh from the society of a treaty-port community, where he has been instructed to regard every Japanese as an inferior being, an object of tolerance at best, the traveller from Europe or America, nevertheless, finds himself asking his *jinrikisha*-drawer or his baggage-carrier to identify some wayside flower new to alien eyes. It does not occur to him that a parallel act in his own country would be to consult a cab driver about ornithological terms or a railway porter about scenic beauties. Yet in Japan the query is generally justified by a correct answer. The rag man, the scavenger, the char-coal-burner, the maid-of-all-work devote some of the spare moments of their unlovely lives to the courtship of flowers, and are more than pleased to communicate the knowledge thus acquired, which is sometimes very considerable.

One expects to find that a people of such tastes have carried to a high point of development the art of rural existence; that from end to end their land is dotted with picturesque dwellings standing among bright blossoms and many-tinted foliage. There is nothing of the kind. If we except the suburban residences of the aristocrats of old times and the plutocrats of modern, no evidence appears to show that life outside the cities has any special charms for the Japanese, or that they appreciate the delights of what is known in the West as a "country house." The big farmers — who, it should be noted, were not originally owners but only tenants of the land they tilled — did occasionally surround themselves with some of the accessories always desired under similar circumstances in the West. But it cannot be said that they ever thought of having mansions, parks, lakes or groves in the Occidental sense of the terms. There were, in fact, no great estates that could be alienated at will or handed down from father to son through long generations. The farmer's house remained a farmer's house, and never assumed the aspect of a wealthy land owner's home. Security of tenure existed as a matter of practice, though not as a matter of right. The feudal chief, whose fief was in effect an heirloom so long as his arm was strong and so long as he neither failed in the duties of vassalage nor incited hostile intrigue by immoral excesses, appreciated the advantage of leaving his tenants undisturbed from generation to generation. Not fear of ejectment, therefore, prevented the farmer from devoting a part of his land to landscape gardening or flower culture on an extended scale. The deterrents were a practical consideration that his holding was taxed in the full ratio of its productive capacity, and a sentimental principle that, after all, he was only a farmer. It is not in the genius of the Japanese that a man should simulate a station not belonging to him or endeavor to seem what he is not. There are trifling exceptions to the wholesome rule. Many women, for example, and some men dye their hair. Tens of thousands of boxes of a peculiarly convenient powder, an import from the omnipotent West, are sent out yearly from the cities to the provinces, and many decoctions from the leaf of a shrub possessing similar properties used to simmer once a month on braziers in the days of Japan's seclusion, and continue to simmer in rarer instances today. Yet there is not a user of the vulgar powder or of the more costly paste that will profess an age even one year below the truth. The physical concealment of time's touches is purely objective; a concession to appearances. Sanemori blackened his hair, nine centuries ago, lest young men should hesitate to cross swords with him in battle.

If Japanese women of this nineteenth century sometimes hide premature streaks of silver, it is because such things obtrude unpleasantly upon the observation of friends and acquaintances. If Japanese men occasionally do the same, it is through fear of being set aside as incapacitated for active employment. But neither man nor woman perpetrates the shocking solecism of arraying age in the garments of youth. A spinster aping the show and the simper of girlhood has no representative in Japan. So, too, the farmer lives outwardly the life of a farmer; the merchant, that of a merchant; the artisan, that of an artisan.

Merely to be wealthy does not — or, at any rate, did not in former times — confer a title to assume the recognized environment of wealth. Hence the castle of the feudal chief, with its generally spacious and always artistically designed park, was the only evidence of opulent and refined life in provincial districts until foreigners came and set the example of erecting, at sites remote from places of business, houses entirely unsuggestive of their occupants' employment, or designed solely for the enjoyment of scenic and seaside pleasures. The fashion appealed at once to the fancy of the Japanese. They wondered that its advantages had not occurred to them before, and to possess a *besso* in the hills or on the coast soon became a

TEA-HOUSE, HOMMOKU, YOKOHAMA.

mark of independent fortune. But these buildings are, without exception, unpretentious. Mere temporary residences, their appearance is in conformity with their subordinate uses. Besides, they are still comparatively few. For the bulk of the people there continues to be only one ideal of holiday or rural existence — life at a spa. The land abounds with thermal springs. Many of them well up among delightful scenery, and about their healing waters picturesque villages have gradually been built, assemblages of inns, where accommodation fitted for all ranks and adapted to all incomes can be obtained. This absence of every evidence of luxurious existence outside the great cities suggests an exaggerated conception of the paltriness of the people's resources, and is doubtless one of the reasons that have induced several foreign observers to describe the Japanese as an essentially poor nation, and to infer an unusual want of material comfort in their home lives. Poor they certainly are, according to the standard of Occidental opulence, and comparatively comfortless must be the existence of any people who inhabit flimsy wooden houses with inner walls of paper; who, instead of sitting in the bright glow of coal or wood fires, cower over charcoal braziers, and who sleep with their heads pillowed upon blocks of wood instead of piles of feathers. But to conclude that Japanese homes lack the paraphernalia of a highly refined civilization, or are without the most logical of all comforts, suitability to the mode of life dictated by the climate, by the products of the soil, and by the physiographical conditions of the country, would be an error into which readers of this volume, at any rate, shall not be betrayed. Upon entering the house of a Japanese gentleman, the foreign visitor of to-day is at first disconcerted by the entire absence of all that he is accustomed to regard as essential to domestic comfort. There are no chairs or other furniture in the reception room, and if he dines with his host the meal will be served upon the floor. If he remains over night he will find no bedstead or other furniture in his sleeping apartment, and as he bestows himself between the comforters upon the floor for slumber, he will no doubt have much the same sensations that he experiences in his own country when he enjoys a comfortable bivouac. Not only are the ordinary appliances for comfort, as he understands it, entirely lacking, but the outward signs of artistic refinement, at first glance, do not appear. There are no pictures, books, bric-a-brac or other movable ornaments such as he is accustomed to find in Occidental homes — merely a general barrenness that seems cold and uninviting. Nevertheless a more intimate acquaintance with his surroundings will tend not only to remove this impression, but to supplant it with the conviction that the exquisite taste expressed by the simple means employed is of a very high order, and that so far as physical comfort is concerned the appliances used are fairly well adapted to the requirements of the Japanese, even though they fail to satisfy Occidental needs.

THE EARLY JAPANESE AND THEIR HISTORY.

EW problems present greater difficulties than that of tracing the origin of the Japanese people back through ages of which the surviving records lack historical accuracy or trustworthiness. Whether the race now inhabiting the islands should be regarded as autochthonous or alien; whether it may not be even an amalgam of various nationalities; if alien, to what parent stock it belonged, and how or at what era it found its way to Japan,—these are unsettled questions that have perplexed anthropologists for many years, and continue to supply food for discussion. It might reasonably be anticipated, arguing from the analogy of other nations, that among the Japanese themselves a definite theory would exist; that tradition would have supplied for them a proud creed, identifying their forefathers with some of the earth's renowned peoples. It might also be contended that, if the progenitors of the nimblewitted, active-bodied, refined and high-spirited folk now bidding so earnestly for a place in the comity of great nations, had migrated originally from a land peopled by men possessing such excellent qualities as they themselves have for centuries displayed, many annals descriptive of that primeval home would have been handed down, however dimly, through the ages. There are no such annals, no such traditions. Fifteen hundred years ago, when the Japanese first learned to record their ideas in writing, and when they undertook to explain their own origin, so unfettered were they by any ethnographic evidences or acknowledged beliefs that they immediately had recourse to the supernatural and derived themselves from heaven. In the earliest times, their historians gravely related, a section of the gods that dwelt upon high Olympus, *Takama no hara*, or the plains of high heaven, descended to an unidentified place called Himuka, and thence gradually pushing eastward, established themselves in the land of sunrise, making the province of Yamato their seat of administration. It is impossible to be at once more sublime and more prosaic than this transition from the empyrean to a vulgar geographical denomination. Western readers will ask at once if the Japanese of to-day credit such a story of their origin. To that the average Japanese of to-day has been known to reply: "Who are you that ask? Have you not had your own burning bush, your own Mount Sinai, your own immaculate conception? Can you conscientiously undertake to rationalize my history while your own contains so much that is irrational?" Behind that *tu quoque*, however, there undoubtedly lurks in the inner

JINRIKISHAS.

The two-wheeled vehicle known as a jinrikisha, drawn by a man, is the ordinary and almost exclusive mode of conveyance in Japan. Horses are seldom used except in the army, and occasionally in agriculture. Two-wheeled drays pushed and pulled by coolies carry heavy loads through the cities and along the country roads. Human labor in Japan is cheaper than equine, and therefore the jinrikisha is in great demand. There are over 250,000 of them in daily use in Japan, and they may be hired by the day for seventy-five sens, or about forty cents in gold. For this sum the "rickshaw" man will patiently trot from 25 to 30 miles per day, exhibiting an endurance that is both cheerful and pathetic.

The invention of the jinrikisha, somewhere about 1867, has been credited by foreign residents to an American missionary named Goble. The natives say that in 1868 a paralytic old gentleman of Kyoto finding his palanquin uncomfortable, built for himself a little cart which was the prototype of the present vehicle. In either case the jinrikisha has been in use for less than thirty years.

consciousness of the educated and intelligent Japanese a resolve not to scrutinize these things too closely. Whether or no the age of the gods, the *Kami-no-yo*, of which, as a child, he read with implicit credence, and of which, as a man, he recognizes the political uses, should be openly relegated to the limbo of absurdities, he finds no pressing reasons to

inquire. Whether the deities had to take part in an immodest dance in order to lure the sun goddess from her cave; whether the god of impulse fought with the god of fire on the shores of the island of the nine provinces; whether the procreative divinities were inspired by a bird; whether the germs of a new civilization were carried across the sea by a prince begotten of the sunshine and born in the shape of a crimson jewel,— these are not problems that call for very serious solution. They are rather allegories from which emerges the serviceable political doctrine that the Emperor of Japan, being of divine origin, rules by divine right. It is the Japanese historian's method, or the Japanese mythologist's manner, of describing an attribute claimed until very recently by all Occidental sovereigns, and still asserted on behalf of some.

Many things are told about these heaven-descended folk who peopled Japan hundreds of years before the Christian era,

and they are things that must be studied by any one desiring to acquaint himself with the motives of Japanese decorative art, for there they play a picturesque and prominent part. But they need not be related here, having already filled many pages in the volumes of other writers. What more concerns us is the fact that the *Takama-no-hara* immigrants did not find an uninhabited country. They found men already dwelling there, men immensely inferior to the newcomers, for these had their chiefs, their officials and their commoners; employed fighting tactics that were apparently invincible, and represented a type of civilization very high for so remote an era. Japanese history, which began to be written in the reign of the Emperor Richu (A. D. 400), traditionally supposed to be the seventeenth in descent from the first mortal sovereign, Jimmu, seems to suggest that several tribes of aborigines resisted the settlement of the heaven-descended immigrants; for we find the autochthons variously designated as *Tsuchigumo* (earth spiders), *Yatsuka haji* (giants), *Kuzu* (moor-men), and *Sauki* (raiders). It has indeed been inferred by some critics that there was question here not merely of different tribes of the same race, but of different races. The generally accepted conclusion, however, used to be that only one race inhabited the islands at the time of the coming of the *Takama no hara* immigrants, and that it was the race called the *Yezo* in early Japanese annals, but now represented by the *Ainu*, a flat-faced, heavy-jawed, tawny-tinged, hirsute people, of whom a little remnant survives in the northern island, called by their name, Yezo, and known to Japanese of the *Meiji* era as Hokkaido. It will be shown presently that there are cogent reasons for querying the theory that the *Yezo*, or *Ainu*, were the sole inhabitants found by the so-called "heavenly visitors" in Japan. For the sake of lucidity, however, two questions had better be considered at once: who were the *Ainu* originally, and were they the primeval dwellers in Japan, or had they also predecessors?

To answer the former question a reference to physiological conditions is helpful. Looking at a map of eastern Asia, it is seen that only some eight miles of sea separate Yezo from Saghalien. The interval was probably wider in early ages, for Japan has long been subject to secular movements. Her coasts are gradually raising themselves from the sea. The same is true of Saghalien. Hence, forty or fifty centuries ago, the Strait of La Pérouse may have measured more than it does now. But the difference can scarcely have been sufficient to affect the possibilities of human immigration. Then, as now, a severe winter meant that the watery interval was frozen over completely, so as to offer easy passage for man or beast. Another glance at the map shows that from Saghalien to the Amur district, across the Gulf of Tartary, is also a mere step. There, too, from time immemorial, the ice has been in the habit of building frequent bridges. It is a reasonable inference that people of the Asiatic continent, finding themselves within reach of the Amur littoral, and finding, also, a safe path across the sea, would have obeyed the instinct that always drives the inhabitants of the bleak north towards the genial south, and, passing over to Saghalien, would thence have pushed on to Yezo, and from Yezo would ultimately have reached the main island of Nippon and the island of Kiushu, still farther south. This geographical suggestion is borne out by ethnographical research, which identifies the *Yezo* with the Arctic tribes of northeastern Asia, whom Rittich groups together as Hyperboreans. But there is nothing in the nature of things to suggest that the *Ainu* were the first to cross from the Asiatic continent to the Japanese islands; nothing to warrant the supposition that they had not been preceded by another race of emigrants; perhaps by many other races. In point of fact, traditions preserved among the *Ainu*, and pit-dwellings and shell-mounds discovered at various places in Japan, indicate that a distinct race had its home in the country before the coming of the *Ainu*. They were the *Koropok-guru*, or pit-dwellers, believed to be represented to-day by some of the inhabitants of Saghalien, the Kuriles and southern Kamtchatka. These semisavages were completely driven out of Japan by the *Aïnu*, no intermixture appearing to have taken place. The *Aïnu* themselves lived in caves, wore long beards, and exhibited the propensities of birds of prey, all of which attributes may be inferred from the names given to them in ancient Japanese annals. The immeasurable superiority of the *Takama-no-hara* immigrants doubtless suggested the legend of their heavenly *provenance*. They knew how to forge spears, swords and knives out of iron; they used bows with feathered arrows; they understood the fire drill and the wedge; they wove hempen cloth; dressed elaborately, their wardrobe including skirts, trousers, girdles, veils, hats, necklaces, bracelets and jeweiled head ornaments; they combed and arranged their hair; they dwelt in wooden houses of solid and tolerably comfortable construction; they rode on horseback; kept cattle, dogs and fowl; lived on flesh, fish and rice, and included chopsticks, cooking pots, cups and dishes among their household utensils. To these invaders the *Yezo* either submitted and became servants, or resisted and were harried with sword, spear and arrow, until, in the seventeenth century of the Christian era, the last of them had been driven from Japan proper to a precarious residence in the northern island. There a gradual extermination, the inevitable fate of the unfit, steadily befell them, so that at the present time only a few thousands remain of a race that must once have numbered millions.

Did the contact of the *Aïnu* with the *Takama-no-hara* invaders leave any permanent mark upon the latter? Was there any blending of the two races? If these questions can be answered in the affirmative, then there will be interest in considering the correlated problem whether the *Aïnu* themselves had been physiologically modified by intercourse with their predecessors, the *Koro-bok-guru*. If the answer be negative, the inquiry need not extend any far-

GIANT PINE TREE AT KARASAKI.

ther, since our subject is not obsolete Japan, to which the remnant of the moribund *Aïnu* race belongs, but Japan of the nineteenth century. By the Japanese themselves it is stoutly affirmed that not the smallest mark of consanguinity can be traced between them and the *Aïnu*, or *Yezo* tribe. Unquestionably the languages of the two have nothing appreciable in common, and so far as outward appearance is concerned, the dissimilarity is conspicuous. Nevertheless, certain German anthropologists have placed on record their opinion that the *Ainu* are Mongolians, and that they differ less from the Japanese than the Germans themselves differ from the Armenians. For purposes of academical investigation that view has doubtless some interest. But practical men naturally ask this question: If, after inhabiting the same country during twenty-five centuries, the hirsute, dusky and conspicuously dirty *Ainu* remains so radically unlike the smooth-faced, comparatively fair-complexioned and scrupulously cleanly Japanese, how many centuries of centuries must have been required to differentiate the two peoples originally, supposing them to have had a common stock, as Doenitz, Hilgendorf and Scheube assert? Were it possible to push research back to the fountain head, it might perhaps be found that all peoples on the face of the globe belonged at one epoch to one family; but the discovery of their primordial relation could only accentuate their present differences. We may accept it as an established fact that the Japanese and the *Ainu* have no affinity whatever.

But the Japanese themselves are not a pure race. They present two easily distinguishable types, the plebeian and the patrician. This is not a question of mere coarseness in contrast with refinement; of the degeneration due to toil and exposure as compared with the improvement produced by gentle living and mental cultivation. The representative of the Japanese plebs has a conspicuously dark skin, prominent cheek bones, a large mouth, a robust and heavily boned physique, a flat nose, full, straight eyes, and a receding forehead. The aristocratic type is symmetrically and delicately built; his complexion varies from yellow to almost pure white; his eyes are narrow, set obliquely to the nose; the eyelids heavy; the eyebrows lofty; the mouth small; the face oval; the nose aquiline; the hand remarkably slender and supple.

Here are two radically distinct types. What is more, they have been distinguished by the Japanese themselves ever since any method of recording such distinctions existed. Confident mention has been made above of the degree of civilization to which the so-called *Takama-no-hara* immigrants had attained fifteen or sixteen centuries ago. Our information in that direction is obtained from two remarkable works, the *Kojiki*, or records of ancient matters, compiled in the year 711 of the Christian era; and the *Nihongi*, a chronicle of Japan, compiled nine years later. The art of writing, as practised in Japan, had been known for about three centuries when these two books were composed. Whatever may be their accuracy or inaccuracy with regard to the incidents of a past already remote at the time of their authors' labors, they certainly furnish a fairly trustworthy account of the state of the country and its people during the early centuries of the Christian era. From them all modern historians have agreed to deduce facts about the civilization of ancient Japan. On the other hand, the antiquity of the pictorial art furnishes information about the physical characteristics of the people. This clew does not lead us quite so far back, it is true, as do the pages of the *Kojiki* and the *Nihongi*, but it does take us to grounds for asserting that, from the very outset, the Japanese artist recognized and depicted only one type of male and female beauty, namely, that distinguished in a marked, often an exaggerated, degree by the features enumerated above as distinctive of the patrician class. There has been no evolution in this matter. The painter had as clear a conception of his type ten centuries ago as he had in the days of Harunobu or Hokusai. Nothing seems more natural than the supposition that this higher type represents the finally dominant race of immigrants, the so-called denizens of *Takama-no-hara*, especially as it is to be found chiefly among the *shizoku*, or military class, whereas the markedly lower type is seen principally among the *heimin*, the fishing, agricultural and trading population. We have to conclude, then, that two tides of immigration reached Japan independently of the *Koro-pok-guru* and the *Ainu*, and it follows, of course, that the inferior race preceded the superior. Here the map again comes to our assistance. Just as Japan is practically connected on the north with the Amur district of the Asiatic continent, so, on the south, the chain of islands to which she belongs, stretches to the Malayan peninsula, and the continuity is further assisted, for purposes of communication, by a current, called the Kuro-shiwo, setting from the Philippines towards Kiushiu. Nothing is more probable than that Malayan adventurers found their way from island to island until they reached Japan, and that they had already peopled its southern parts, driving out any Ainu found there, when the so-called *Takama-no-hara* invaders appeared upon the scene. The Malayan type and the Japanese plebeian type are sufficiently similar to confirm that hypothesis. It remains, then, to discover the origin of the *Takama-no-hara* immigrants.

Japanese history commences with the Emperor Jimmu, who in 663 B.C. is said to have set out from a place called Mimizu, on the east coast of Kiushiu, and, after an immensely protracted voyage, to have reached the Bay of Osaka. Landing there, he subdued the neighboring districts, and established himself in Yamato province. Independently of the fact that Japanese annals did not begin to be written until more than a thousand years after the

alleged date of Jimmu's adventures, there are internal evidences that impair the credibility of this early history. But the main facts, namely, that an invader arrived over sea, that he established the Japanese dynasty, and that he was accompanied by the forefathers of the thenceforth dominant race, may be accepted as true. Western ethnologists are tolerably agreed that Jimmu and his followers were Mongolians. There have been attempts to identify them with the lost tribes of Israel; with the Aztecs and with other peoples of the Occident. In Japan there is a belief that they were Manchurians; that is to say, a race which originally emigrated from a remote part of India, a race distinct from the Chinese, of which some settled in Manchuria, spread thence to the northeast of China, and finally passed to Japan. It must be agreed, for the moment, to leave the problem partially unsolved; noting, however, that though the Japanese *shizoku* cannot be absolutely identified with the Mongolian race of today, the differences are not so great as to be incapable of reference to the modifying influences of environment acting throughout long centuries. At all events, we may conclude that the final immigrants, Jimmu and his followers, or the so-called *Takama-no-hara* folk, found, on their arrival, a Malayan people inhabiting the southern and central parts of Japan, and an Arctic tribe, the *Ainu*, living in the north, and that, while they amalgamated with the former after conquest, they drove out the latter, treating them as a wholly inferior race, the result being that whereas the Japanese proper show plainly enough the blending of the Mongolian and Malayan types, they show no affinity whatever with the *Ainu*.

These conclusions do not embrace all the suggestions furnished by tradition and physiography. We have accepted the probability that Arctic tribes found their way to Japan along the chain of islands lying between the mouth of the Amur and the Tsugaru Strait; that a tropical tribe migrated northward via the Philippines, Formosa and the Riukiu archipelago; and that a band of Mongolian conquerors arrived over sea. But at another point, also, there exists between Japan and the Asiatic continent a practicable route, namely, from the Korean peninsula by the islands known as Matsushima (Dagelet), the Liancourts and Okishima, or by Tsushima, Iki and Matsuura. The last of the former three stepping-stones would have brought Korean adventurers within a few miles of the Japanese district of Izumo. Now Izumo figures very prominently in the traditions that the authors of the *Kojiki* and the *Nihongi* applied themselves to record.

When something like consistency emerges from the web of myths and allegories into which unlettered tradition wove the annals of Japan's earliest peoples, attention is immediately directed to Izumo as the seat of government. Before that time, the background of history is occupied by mystic figures of deities whose very titles are abstractions, until at last the God and Goddess of Procreation (*Izanagi* and *Izanami*) having begotten the islands of the Japanese archipelago, beget, afterwards, personifications of the natural phenomena whose operation is to render the islands inhabitable. *Izanami* dies in giving birth to fire. Prometheus-like, she purchases with her life this priceless gift to mortals. *Izanagi*, the Orpheus of Japanese mythology, pays a profitless visit to the land of the shades in search of his deceased spouse, and then himself assumes her functions as a child-bearer. From his left eye emerges the Goddess of the Sun, from his right the God of the Moon, and from his nose the Deity of Impulse, *Susanoo*. To these three the empire of the universe is bequeathed by their sire. But they fight among themselves, and it is not till five generations of *Izanagi's* descendants have come and gone that he nominates the first-born of the sixth to the sovereignty of Japan. This monarch settles in Izumo. He apparently represents the chieftain of a band of adventurers who immigrated from the direction of Korea. By-and-by, another tide of immigration, this time setting from the south, and composed, we may assume, of the Mongoloid wanderers already spoken of, reaches the shores of Kiushu, and a struggle ensues between the newcomers and the children of the Deity of Impulse. The second immigrants seem to have been worshippers of the Sun, for the God of that orb, *Susanoo's* brother, is their patron. A pact is at last arranged by the heavenly intervention of the disputants' common ancestor. The Izumo rulers abdicate in favor of the invaders, and in the sixth century before our era, Jimmu Tennô, the so-called founder of the Imperial dynasty of Japan, is established in the province of Yamato, as undisputed ruler of the south and centre, though farther north his authority long continues to be resisted by the *Ainu*.

Jimmu, though everything that concerns him is wrapped in the obscurity of prehistoric times, has great interest for students of Japanese life and thought, since the story of his doings, as constructed by the first of his country's annalists thirteen centuries later, shows at least the kind of hero that men of subsequent generations were disposed to depict as the founder of the sacred dynasty, the chief of the Japanese race. The youngest of four sons, he was nevertheless selected by his father to succeed to the rulership of the little colony of invaders then settled in Kiushu, and his elder brothers obediently recognized this right of choice. Hiko Hohodemi, or Sanu, as the hero was then called, is represented in the light of a kind of viking. Learning of a delectable land in the east, inhabited by semi-barbarous

tribes whose primitive arms were incapable of offering any effective resistance to his trained braves, he embarked all his available forces in war vessels, and set out upon a tour of aggression. Creeping along the eastern shore of Kiushu, and finally entering the Inland Sea, the adventurers fought their way from point to point, landing sometimes to do battle with native tribes, sometimes to construct new war junks, until, after seven years of fighting and wandering, they finally emerged from the northern end of the Inland Sea and established themselves in Yamato, destined to be thenceforth the Imperial province of Japan. In this long series of campaigns, the chieftain lost his three brothers: one fell in fight; two threw themselves into the sea to calm a tempest that threatened to destroy the flotilla. Such are the deaths that Japanese in all ages have regarded as ideal exits from this mortal scene—deaths by the sword and deaths of loyal self-sacrifice. To the leader himself after his decease, the posthumous name of Jimmu, or "the man of divine bravery," was given, typifying the honor that has always attached to the profession of arms in Japan. The distance from this primitive viking's starting point to the place where he established his capital and consummated his career of conquest, can easily be traversed by a modern steamer in three times as many hours as the number of years devoted by Jimmu and his followers to the task. That the craft in which they travelled were of the most inefficient type, may be gathered from the fact that the viking's progress eastward would have been finally interrupted by the narrow strip of water dividing Kiushu from the main island of Japan, had not a fisherman seated on a turtle emboldened him to strike seaward. Thenceforth the turtle assumed a leading place in the mythology of Japan—the type of longevity, the messenger of the marine deity who dwelt in the crystal depths of the ocean, his palace peopled by lovely maidens. The Goddess of the Sun shone on his enterprise at times when tempest or fog threatened serious peril, and a kite circling overhead indicated the direction of inhabited districts when he and his warriors had lost their way among mountains and forests. How much of all this was transmitted by tradition to the writers of Jimmu's history in the eighth century; how much was a mere reflection of national customs which had then become sacred, and on which the political scholars of the time desired to set the seal of antique sanction, who shall determine? If Sanu and his warriors brought with them the worship of the sun, that would offer an interesting inference as to their origin. If the aid that they received from his light was suggested solely by the grateful homage that rice cultivators, thirteen centuries later, had learned to pay to his beneficence, the *Kojiki* and the *Nihongi* must be read as mere transcripts of the faiths and fashions of the era when they were written, not as records of previous ages. But such distinctions have never been recognized by the Japanese. With them these annals of their race's beginnings have always commanded as inviolable credence as the testaments of Christianity used to command in the Occident.

www.ingramcontent.com/pod-product-compliance
Lightning Source LLC
Chambersburg PA
CBHW032135080426
42733CB00008B/1086